Contents

The following sample exam paper is a printed representation of how this exam will appear when online. The structure of the questions, the knowledge required and the topics covered will be the same. However, in order to suit an online platform, the wording of the questions and the method of answering them may be different.

Terminology:

bar	breve	semibreve	minim	crotchet	quaver	semiquaver	demisemiquaver
measure	double whole note	whole note	half note	quarter note	8th note	16th note	32nd note

1 Rhythm

/10

1.1 Circle the correct time signature for each of these bars.

(3)

(a)	$\frac{2}{4}$	$\frac{7}{8}$	$\frac{5}{8}$

(b)	$\frac{2}{4}$	$\frac{5}{8}$	$\frac{9}{16}$

(c)	$\frac{7}{8}$	$\frac{6}{8}$	$\frac{3}{4}$

1.2 Here is a bar in simple time:

(1)

Which of the following shows the bar above correctly rewritten in compound time? Tick (✔) **one** box.

 ☐

 ☐

 ☐

1.3 Complete the following **two** sentences by adding a number to each.

(2)

(a) In $\frac{6}{4}$ there are .... dotted-minim beats in a bar.

(b) A dotted-quaver is equal to .... semiquaver(s).

1.4 Tick (✔) **one** box to show which bar is grouped correctly.

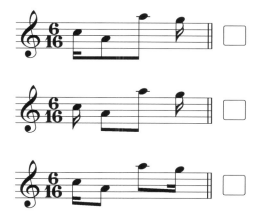

1.5 Tick (✔) or cross (✘) **each** box to show whether the rests are correct **or** incorrect. (3)

2.1 Tick (✔) **one** box to show the name of this note. (1)

 A ☐ B ☐ D ☐ G ☐

2.2 Tick (✔) **one** box to show the correct enharmonic equivalent of this note. (1)

  ☐  ☐  ☐

2.3 Here is a bar written for the horn in F. (5)

This bar has been transposed down a perfect 5th to be at sounding pitch. There are some mistakes. Put a tick (✔) **or** cross (✘) underneath the key signature and each note to show whether each is correct **or** incorrect.

☐ ☐ ☐ ☐ ☐

2.4 Compare bars **A**, **B** and **C**, then circle **TRUE** or **FALSE** for each of the **three** statements. (3)

A  B C

(a) **A** and **B** are at the same pitch   **TRUE**   **FALSE**

(b) **A** is one octave higher than **C**   **TRUE**   **FALSE**

(c) **B** is one octave higher than **C**   **TRUE**   **FALSE**

3 Keys and Scales

3.1 Tick (✔) **one** box to show the correctly written key signature of G♭ major. (1)

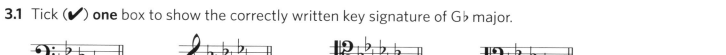

☐   ☐   ☐   ☐

3.2 Tick (✔) **one** box to show the correctly written key signature of D♯ minor. (1)

☐   ☐   ☐   ☐

3.3 Circle the correct key of each of these **three** melodies. (3)

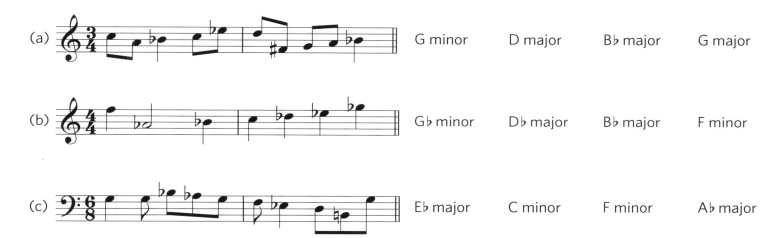

(a) G minor   D major   B♭ major   G major

(b) G♭ minor   D♭ major   B♭ major   F minor

(c) E♭ major   C minor   F minor   A♭ major

3.4 Tick (✔) **one box for X** and **one box for Y** to show which notes are needed (2)
to complete the scale of **A major**

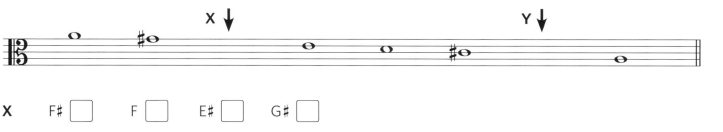

X   F♯ ☐   F ☐   E♯ ☐   G♯ ☐

Y   B♯ ☐   A ☐   B ☐   C ☐

3.5 Circle **one** clef for each scale, to form **minor** scales. (3)

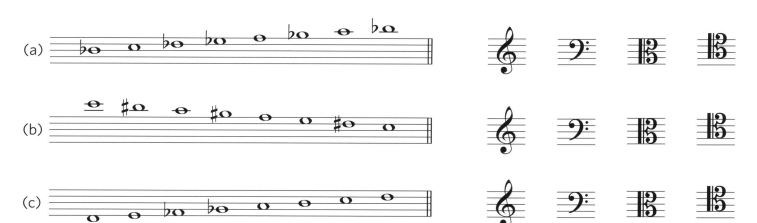

(a)

(b)

(c)

3.6 Circle **TRUE** or **FALSE** for each statement. (2)

(a) This is the correctly written chromatic scale beginning on B♭   **TRUE**   **FALSE**

(b) This is the correctly written chromatic scale beginning on D   **TRUE**   **FALSE**

3.7 Circle **TRUE** or **FALSE** for each statement. (3)

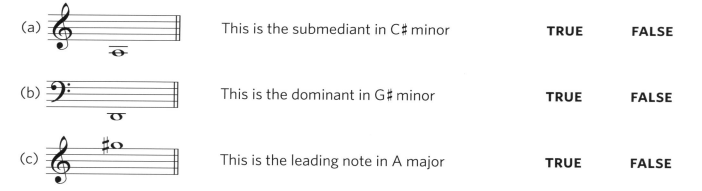

(a)   This is the submediant in C♯ minor   **TRUE**   **FALSE**

(b)   This is the dominant in G♯ minor   **TRUE**   **FALSE**

(c)   This is the leading note in A major   **TRUE**   **FALSE**

4.1 Tick (✔) **one** box to name each interval. (3)

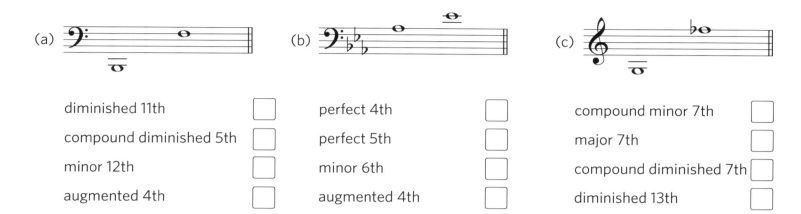

diminished 11th ☐	perfect 4th ☐	compound minor 7th ☐
compound diminished 5th ☐	perfect 5th ☐	major 7th ☐
minor 12th ☐	minor 6th ☐	compound diminished 7th ☐
augmented 4th ☐	augmented 4th ☐	diminished 13th ☐

4.2 Circle the type of each interval. (3)

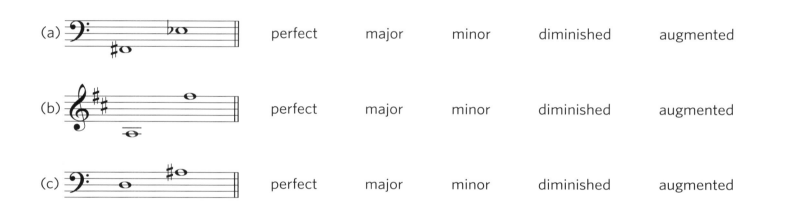

(a)   perfect   major   minor   diminished   augmented

(b)   perfect   major   minor   diminished   augmented

(c)   perfect   major   minor   diminished   augmented

4.3 Write notes to form the named intervals. Your note should be **higher** than the given note. (4)

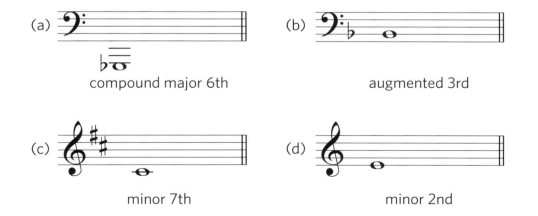

(a) compound major 6th

(b) augmented 3rd

(c) minor 7th

(d) minor 2nd

5 Chords

5.1 Indicate suitable chords in the two cadences in the following melody by writing either I, II, IV or V in each of the **five** boxes underneath the staves.

(5)

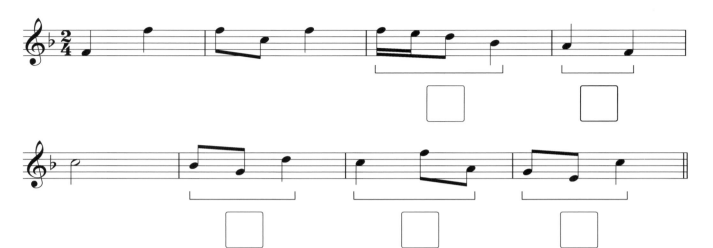

5.2 Tick (✔) **one** box to name each cadence.

(2)

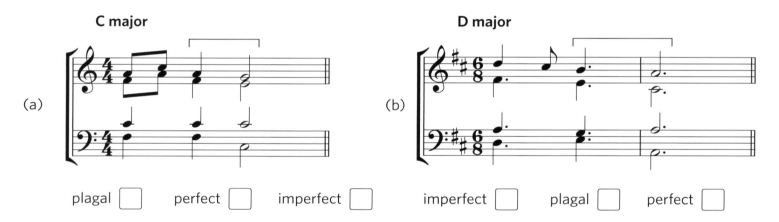

(a)   C major

plagal ☐   perfect ☐   imperfect ☐

(b)   D major

imperfect ☐   plagal ☐   perfect ☐

5.3 Tick (✔) one box to name each of the **three** marked chords. The key is F major.

(3)

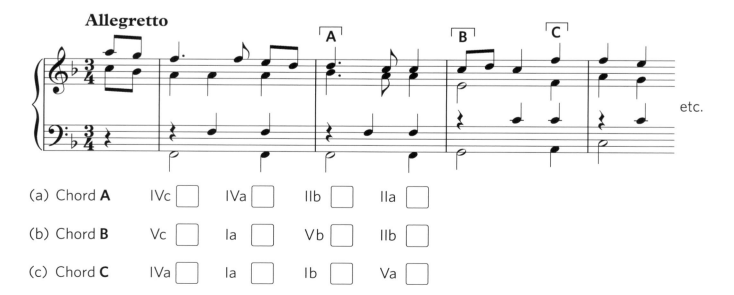

(a) Chord **A**   IVc ☐   IVa ☐   IIb ☐   IIa ☐

(b) Chord **B**   Vc ☐   Ia ☐   Vb ☐   IIb ☐

(c) Chord **C**   IVa ☐   Ia ☐   Ib ☐   Va ☐

6 Terms, Signs and Instruments

/10

6.1 Tick (✔) **one** box for each term/sign. (3)

vite means:

fairly quick ☐
playful, joking ☐
quick ☐
as fast as possible ☐

traurig means:

slow ☐
sad ☐
sweet ☐
simple ☐

perdendosi means:

dying away ☐
playful, merry ☐
calm ☐
with passion ☐

6.2 Tick (✔) one box to name each of the **two** written-out ornaments, which are marked with brackets. (2)

(a)

trill ☐   acciaccatura ☐   lower mordent ☐   appoggiatura ☐

(b)

acciaccatura ☐   upper mordent ☐   turn ☐   trill ☐

6.3 Circle **TRUE** or **FALSE** for each of the following **five** statements. (5)

(a) The violin sometimes uses the alto clef   **TRUE**   **FALSE**

(b) The oboe is the highest-sounding woodwind instrument   **TRUE**   **FALSE**

(c) The trombone has a higher range than the tuba   **TRUE**   **FALSE**

(d) The bassoon is a transposing instrument   **TRUE**   **FALSE**

(e) A viola might be played 'arco'   **TRUE**   **FALSE**

Study this music for violin and piano and then answer the questions that follow.

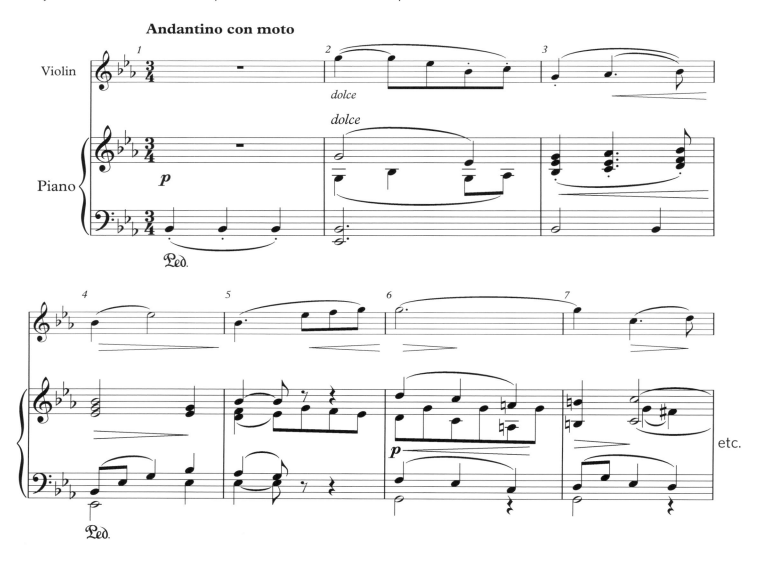

7.1 Compare the following bars to bar 2 of the violin part, then tick (✔) the **one** correct statement.   (1)

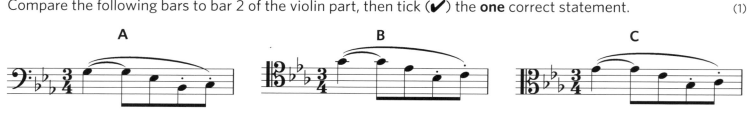

Only **A** and **C** are correctly rewritten two octaves lower   ☐

Only **A** is correctly rewritten two octaves lower   ☐

Only **A** and **B** are correctly rewritten two octaves lower   ☐

A, **B** and **C** are correctly rewritten two octaves lower   ☐

7.2 Circle **TRUE** or **FALSE** for each of the following **five** statements about the music. (5)

    (a) The violin should be played sweetly   **TRUE**   **FALSE**

    (b) G minor is the relative minor key of E♭ major   **TRUE**   **FALSE**

    (c) The widest interval in the violin part is a perfect 4th   **TRUE**   **FALSE**

    (d) The lowest note in the extract is C   **TRUE**   **FALSE**

    (e) The speed of the music is very slow   **TRUE**   **FALSE**

7.3 Which other instrument is best suited to play the violin part so that it sounds at the same pitch? (1)
Tick (✔) **one** box.

    flute ☐   double bass ☐   bassoon ☐   timpani ☐

7.4 How many times does the **submediant** note in the key of E♭ major appear in the violin part? (1)
Tick (✔) **one** box.

    1 ☐   2 ☐   4 ☐   5 ☐

7.5 Complete the following **two** sentences by adding a number to each. (2)

    (a) Bar…………. contains a tonic chord in second inversion, in E♭ major.

    (b) Bar…………. contains a chord of G major.

Total marks: /75

1 Rhythm

/10

1.1 Circle the correct time signature for each of these bars.

(3)

(a)

$\frac{3}{4}$ $\frac{6}{8}$ $\frac{7}{8}$

(b)

$\frac{7}{8}$ $\frac{9}{8}$ $\frac{5}{4}$

(c)

$\frac{6}{4}$ $\frac{6}{8}$ $\frac{3}{2}$

1.2 Here is a bar in compound time:

(1)

Which of the following shows the bar above correctly rewritten in simple time? Tick (✔) **one** box.

 ☐

 ☐

 ☐

1.3 Complete the following **two** sentences by adding a number to each.

(2)

(a) In $\frac{9}{8}$ there are .... dotted-crotchet beats in a bar.

(b) A dotted-minim is equal to .... semiquaver(s).

1.4 Tick (✔) **one** box to show which bar is grouped correctly.

1.5 Tick (✔) **or** cross (✘) **each** box to show whether the rests are correct **or** incorrect.

(3)

2.1 Tick (✔) **one** box to show the name of this note. (1)

   C ☐   G ☐   A ☐   B ☐

2.2 Tick (✔) **one** box to show the correct enharmonic equivalent of this note. (1)

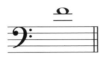    ☐    ☐    ☐

2.3 Here is a bar written for the clarinet in B♭. (5)

This bar has been transposed down a major 2nd to be at sounding pitch. There are some mistakes. Put a tick (✔) **or** cross (✘) underneath the key signature and each note to show whether each is correct **or** incorrect.

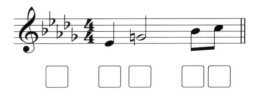

☐   ☐ ☐   ☐ ☐

2.4 Compare bars **A**, **B** and **C**, then circle **TRUE** or **FALSE** for each of the **three** statements. (3)

A    B    C

(a) **A** and **C** are at the same pitch   **TRUE**   **FALSE**

(b) **B** is one octave higher than **A**   **TRUE**   **FALSE**

(c) **C** is one octave lower than **B**   **TRUE**   **FALSE**

3.1 Tick (✔) **one** box to show the correctly written key signature of B♭ minor. (1)

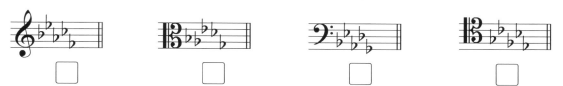

☐ ☐ ☐ ☐

3.2 Tick (✔) **one** box to show the correctly written key signature of B major. (1)

☐ ☐ ☐ ☐

3.3 Circle the correct key of each of these **three** melodies. (3)

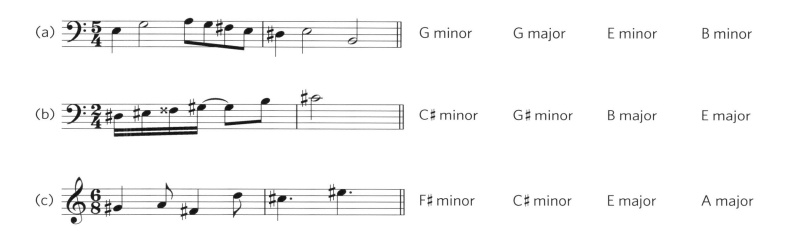

(a) G minor   G major   E minor   B minor

(b) C♯ minor   G♯ minor   B major   E major

(c) F♯ minor   C♯ minor   E major   A major

3.4 Tick (✔) **one box for X** and **one box for Y** to show which notes are needed to complete the scale of **D harmonic minor**. (2)

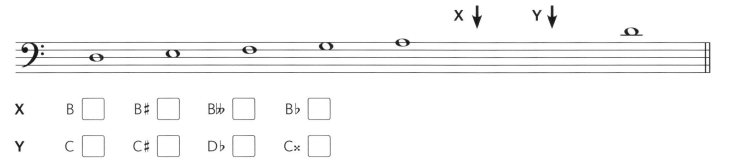

X   B ☐   B♯ ☐   B♭♭ ☐   B♭ ☐

Y   C ☐   C♯ ☐   D♭ ☐   C✕ ☐

3.5 Circle **one** clef for each scale, to form **minor** scales. (3)

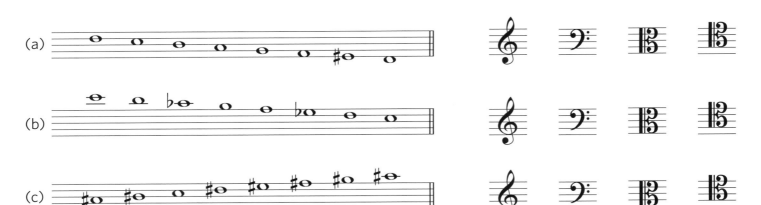

3.6 Circle **TRUE** or **FALSE** for each statement. (2)

(a) This is the correctly written chromatic scale beginning on C♯   **TRUE**   **FALSE**

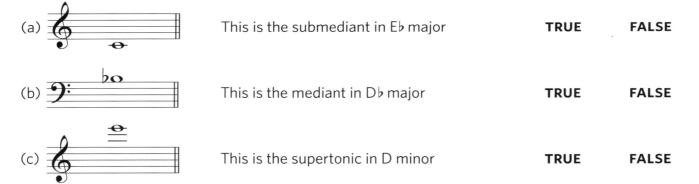

(b) This is the correctly written chromatic scale beginning on E   **TRUE**   **FALSE**

3.7 Circle **TRUE** or **FALSE** for each statement. (3)

(a) This is the submediant in E♭ major   **TRUE**   **FALSE**

(b) This is the mediant in D♭ major   **TRUE**   **FALSE**

(c) This is the supertonic in D minor   **TRUE**   **FALSE**

4 Intervals

4.1 Tick (✔) **one** box to name each interval. (3)

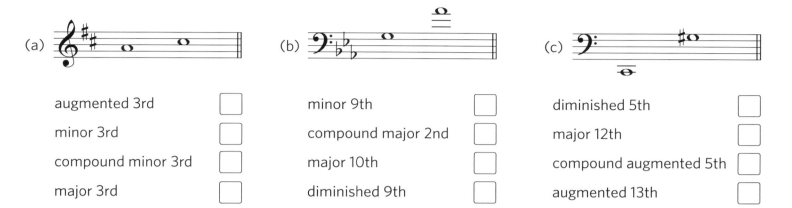

(a)		(b)		(c)	
augmented 3rd	☐	minor 9th	☐	diminished 5th	☐
minor 3rd	☐	compound major 2nd	☐	major 12th	☐
compound minor 3rd	☐	major 10th	☐	compound augmented 5th	☐
major 3rd	☐	diminished 9th	☐	augmented 13th	☐

4.2 Circle the type of each interval. (3)

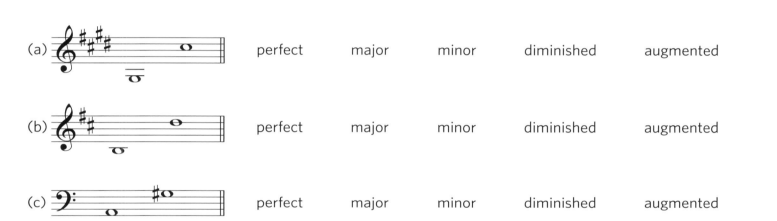

(a)   perfect   major   minor   diminished   augmented

(b)   perfect   major   minor   diminished   augmented

(c)   perfect   major   minor   diminished   augmented

4.3 Write notes to form the named intervals. Your note should be **higher** than the given note. (4)

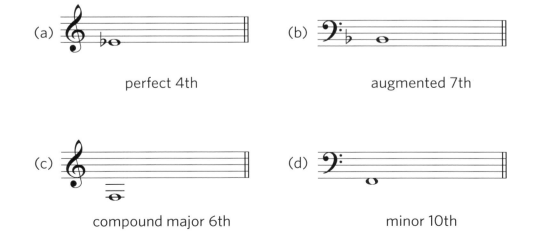

(a) perfect 4th

(b) augmented 7th

(c) compound major 6th

(d) minor 10th

5.1 Indicate suitable chords for the two cadences in the following melody by writing either I, II, IV or V (5)
in each of the **five** boxes underneath the staves.

5.2 Tick (✔) **one** box to name each cadence. (2)

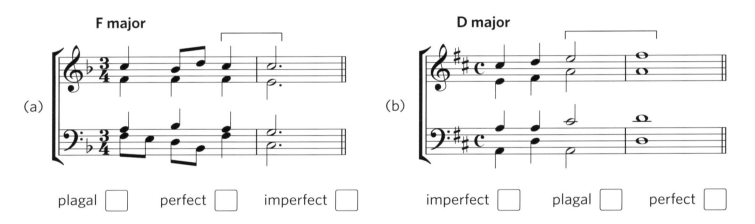

(a) plagal ☐ perfect ☐ imperfect ☐

(b) imperfect ☐ plagal ☐ perfect ☐

5.3 Tick (✔) one box to name each of the **three** marked chords. The key is D major. (3)

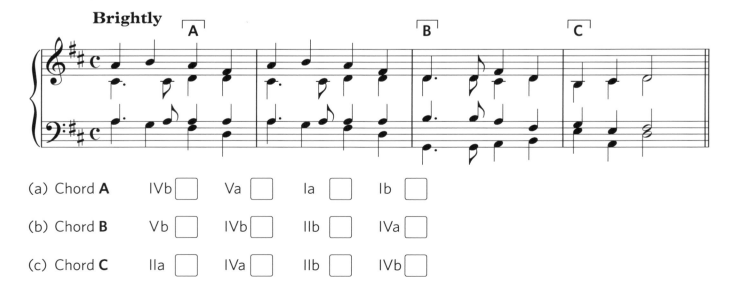

(a) Chord **A** IVb ☐ Va ☐ Ia ☐ Ib ☐

(b) Chord **B** Vb ☐ IVb ☐ IIb ☐ IVa ☐

(c) Chord **C** IIa ☐ IVa ☐ IIb ☐ IVb ☐

6 Terms, Signs and Instruments

6.1 Tick (✔) **one** box for each term/sign. (3)

langsam means:

moderately ☐

dying away ☐

smoothly ☐

slow ☐

sotto voce means:

resonant, with rich tone ☐

in an undertone ☐

with passion ☐

simple, plain ☐

douce means:

sweet ☐

expressive ☐

heavy ☐

smoothly ☐

6.2 Tick (✔) one box to name each of the **two** written-out ornaments, which are marked with brackets. (2)

(a)

trill ☐   turn ☐   lower mordent ☐   appoggiatura ☐

(b)

acciaccatura ☐   trill ☐   turn ☐   upper mordent ☐

6.3 Circle **TRUE** or **FALSE** for each of the following **five** statements. (5)

(a) The violin sometimes uses the alto clef	**TRUE**	**FALSE**
(b) A bass voice has a lower range than a baritone voice	**TRUE**	**FALSE**
(c) The marimba produces sounds of definite pitch	**TRUE**	**FALSE**
(d) The oboe uses a single reed	**TRUE**	**FALSE**
(e) The clarinet is a transposing instrument	**TRUE**	**FALSE**

Study this music and then answer the questions that follow.

7.1 Compare the following bars to bar 8 of the right-hand part, then tick (✔)
the **one** correct statement.

(1)

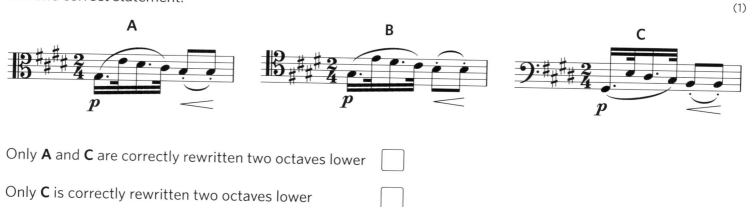

Only **A** and **C** are correctly rewritten two octaves lower ☐

Only **C** is correctly rewritten two octaves lower ☐

Only **B** and **C** are correctly rewritten two octaves lower ☐

A, **B** and **C** are correctly rewritten two octaves lower ☐

7.2 Circle **TRUE** or **FALSE** for each of the following **five** statements about the music. (5)

(a) The music should be played in a singing style   **TRUE**   **FALSE**

(b) There are three acciaccaturas in this melody   **TRUE**   **FALSE**

(c) Bars 1 and 2 of the left-hand part contain all the notes of the tonic triad of E major   **TRUE**   **FALSE**

(d) The lowest note in the extract is D♯   **TRUE**   **FALSE**

(e) C minor has the same key signature as E major   **TRUE**   **FALSE**

7.3 Which other instrument is best suited to play the notes of the right-hand part of bars 1–4 so that they sound (1) at the same pitch? Tick (✔) **one** box.

oboe ☐   bassoon ☐   double bass ☐   tuba ☐

7.4 How many times does the **submediant** note in the key of E major appear in the right-hand part? (1) Tick (✔) **one** box.

3 ☐   6 ☐   7 ☐   8 ☐

7.5 Complete the following **two** sentences by adding a number to each. (2)

(a) The first note in the right-hand part of bar 4 is worth .... demisemiquavers.

(b) There is an instruction to play the notes semi-staccato in bar ....

Music Theory Sample Paper 2020 Grade 5 C

Exam duration: 2 hours maximum

Total marks: /75

1 Rhythm

/10

1.1 Circle the correct time signature for each of these bars.

(3)

(a) $\frac{12}{8}$ $\frac{6}{8}$ $\frac{9}{16}$

(b) $\frac{7}{8}$ $\frac{9}{16}$ $\frac{6}{8}$

(c) $\frac{9}{8}$ C $\frac{12}{16}$

1.2 Here is a bar in compound time:

(1)

Which of the following shows the bar above correctly rewritten in simple time? Tick (✔) **one** box.

1.3 Complete the following **two** sentences by adding a number to each.

(2)

(a) In $\frac{9}{8}$ there are .... dotted-crotchet beats in a bar.

(b) A minim is equal to .... demisemiquaver(s).

1.4 Tick (✔) **one** box to show which bar is grouped correctly. (1)

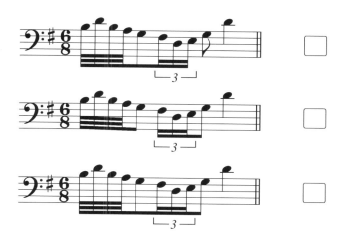

1.5 Tick (✔) or cross (✗) **each** box to show whether the rests are correct **or** incorrect. (3)

2 Pitch /10

2.1 Tick (✔) **one** box to show the name of this note. (1)

 F   B   G   A

2.2 Tick (✔) **one** box to show the correct enharmonic equivalent of this note. (1)

2.3 Here is a bar at sounding pitch for the cor anglais. (5)

This bar has been transposed up a perfect 5th to be at written pitch. There are some mistakes.
Put a tick (✔) **or** cross (✘) underneath the key signature and each note to show whether each is
correct **or** incorrect.

☐ ☐ ☐☐☐

2.4 Compare bars **A**, **B** and **C**, then circle **TRUE** or **FALSE** for each of the **three** statements. (3)

A    B    C

(a) **A** and **C** are at the same pitch   **TRUE**   **FALSE**

(b) **A** is one octave higher than **B**   **TRUE**   **FALSE**

(c) **B** is one octave lower than **C**   **TRUE**   **FALSE**

3.1 Tick (✔) **one** box to show the correctly written key signature of D♯ minor.

(1)

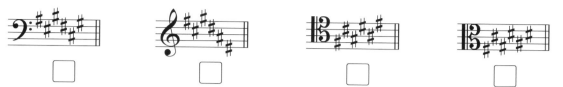

☐   ☐   ☐   ☐

3.2 Tick (✔) **one** box to show the correctly written key signature of G♭ major.

(1)

☐   ☐   ☐   ☐

3.3 Circle the correct key of each of these **three** melodies.

(3)

(a)   B♭ minor   G minor   E♭ major   F minor

(b)   E♭ major   B♭ major   A♭ major   G minor

(c)   E♭ minor   B♭ major   F major   B♭ minor

3.4 Tick (✔) **one box for X** and **one box for Y** to show which notes are needed to complete the scale of D♭ major.

(2)

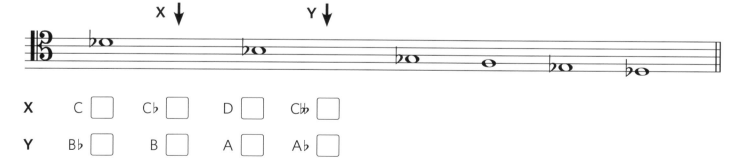

X   C ☐   C♭ ☐   D ☐   C♭ ☐

Y   B♭ ☐   B ☐   A ☐   A♭ ☐

3.5 Circle **one** clef for each scale, to form **minor** scales. (3)

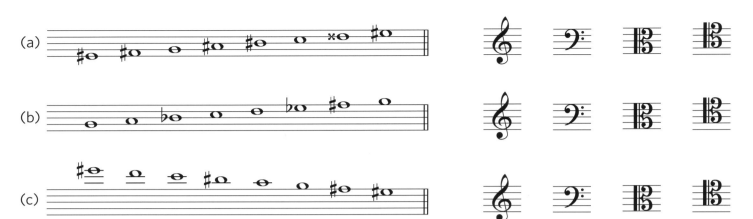

3.6 Circle **TRUE** or **FALSE** for each statement. (2)

(a) This is the correctly written chromatic scale beginning on F   **TRUE**   **FALSE**

(b) This is the correctly written chromatic scale beginning on D♯   **TRUE**   **FALSE**

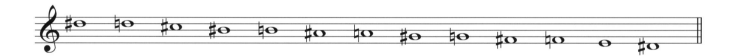

3.7 Circle **TRUE** or **FALSE** for each statement. (3)

(a) This is the subdominant in F minor   **TRUE**   **FALSE**

(b) This is the tonic in B♭ minor   **TRUE**   **FALSE**

(c) This is the supertonic in D major   **TRUE**   **FALSE**

4 Intervals

4.1 Tick (✔) **one** box to name each interval.

(3)

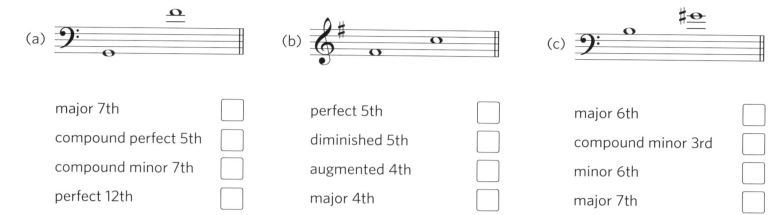

major 7th ☐	perfect 5th ☐	major 6th ☐
compound perfect 5th ☐	diminished 5th ☐	compound minor 3rd ☐
compound minor 7th ☐	augmented 4th ☐	minor 6th ☐
perfect 12th ☐	major 4th ☐	major 7th ☐

4.2 Circle the type of each interval.

(3)

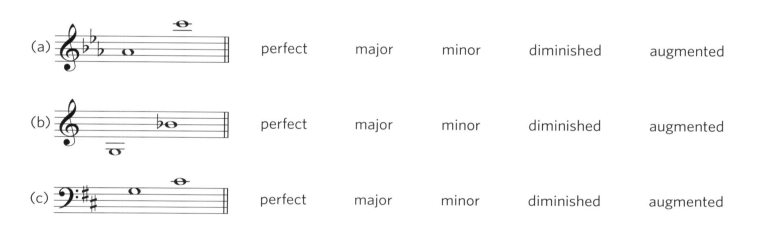

(a)   perfect   major   minor   diminished   augmented

(b)   perfect   major   minor   diminished   augmented

(c)   perfect   major   minor   diminished   augmented

4.3 Write notes to form the named intervals. Your note should be **higher** than the given note.

(4)

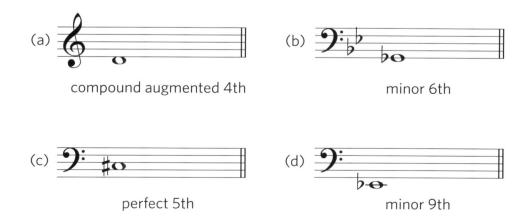

(a) compound augmented 4th

(b) minor 6th

(c) perfect 5th

(d) minor 9th

5 Chords

5.1 Indicate suitable chords for the two cadences in the following melody by writing either I, II, IV or V in each of the **five** boxes underneath the staves.

(5)

5.2 Tick (✔) **one** box to name each cadence.

(2)

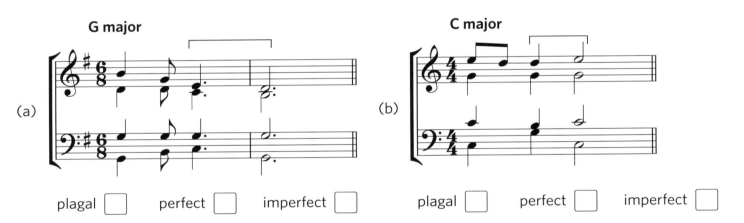

(a)   plagal ☐   perfect ☐   imperfect ☐   (b)   plagal ☐   perfect ☐   imperfect ☐

5.3 Tick (✔) one box to name each of the **three** marked chords. The key is D minor.

(3)

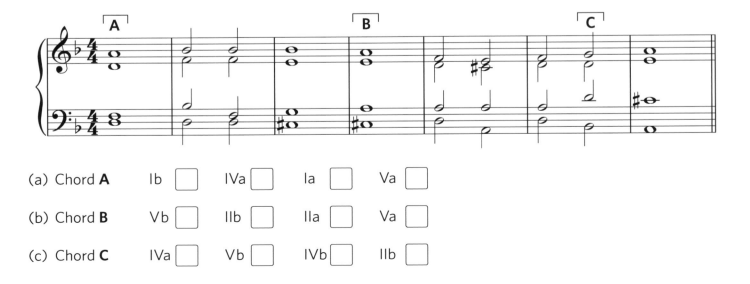

(a) Chord **A**   Ib ☐   IVa ☐   Ia ☐   Va ☐

(b) Chord **B**   Vb ☐   IIb ☐   IIa ☐   Va ☐

(c) Chord **C**   IVa ☐   Vb ☐   IVb ☐   IIb ☐

6 Terms, Signs and Instruments

6.1 Tick (✔) **one** box for each term/sign. (3)

giocoso means:

graceful ☐

playful, merry ☐

rather slow ☐

sweet ☐

perdendosi means:

dying away ☐

heavy ☐

gradually getting louder ☐

agitated ☐

lebhaft means:

getting quicker ☐

always ☐

smooth ☐

lively ☐

6.2 Tick (✔) one box to name each of the **two** written-out ornaments, which are marked with brackets. (2)

(a)

lower mordent ☐   trill ☐   turn ☐   acciaccatura ☐

(b)

appoggiatura ☐   acciaccatura ☐   trill ☐   lower mordent ☐

6.3 Circle **TRUE** or **FALSE** for each of the following **five** statements. (5)

(a) The triangle produces sounds of definite pitch   **TRUE**   **FALSE**

(b) The horn is a transposing instrument   **TRUE**   **FALSE**

(c) The bass drum produces sounds of definite pitch   **TRUE**   **FALSE**

(d) 'Pizzicato' means to play with the bow   **TRUE**   **FALSE**

(e) A flute might be played 'con sord.'   **TRUE**   **FALSE**

7 Music in Context

Study this music for clarinet in B♭ and piano and then answer the questions that follow.

7.1 Compare the following bars to bar 2 of the left-hand piano part, then tick (✔)
the **one** correct statement.

(1)

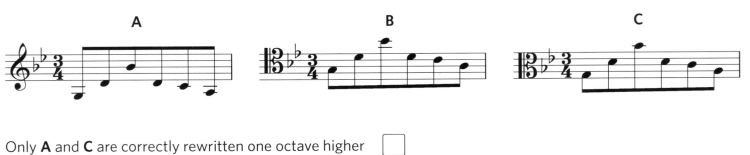

Only **A** and **C** are correctly rewritten one octave higher ☐

Only **B** is correctly rewritten one octave lower ☐

Only **A** and **C** are correctly rewritten one octave lower ☐

A, **B** and **C** are correctly rewritten one octave higher ☐

7.2 Circle **TRUE** or **FALSE** for each of the following **five** statements about the music. (5)

    (a) The music should be played happily   **TRUE**   **FALSE**

    (b) The clarinet in bar 3 should be played in an undertone   **TRUE**   **FALSE**

    (c) The tempo remains the same throughout the melody   **TRUE**   **FALSE**

    (d) The highest note in the piano part is an E   **TRUE**   **FALSE**

    (e) There are three pairs of grace notes in the music   **TRUE**   **FALSE**

7.3 Which instrument is best suited to play the notes of the left-hand piano part in bars 1–5 so that they sound at the same pitch? Tick (✔) **one** box. (1)

    trumpet ☐   viola ☐   oboe ☐   cello ☐

7.4 How many times does the **dominant** note in the key of G minor appear in the left-hand piano part? Tick (✔) **one** box. (1)

    7 ☐   8 ☐   12 ☐   14 ☐

7.5 Complete the following **two** sentences by adding a number to each. (2)

    (a) There is an accent in bar ....

    (b) There is a trill in bar ....

Music Theory Sample Paper 2020 Grade 5 D

Exam duration: 2 hours maximum

1 Rhythm

/10

1.1 Circle the correct time signature for each of these bars.

(3)

7 4   **3 2**   **12 16**

3 2   **9 8**   **12 16**

4 4   **4 2**   **12 8**

1.2 Here is a bar in simple time:

(1)

Which of the following shows the bar above correctly rewritten in compound time? Tick (✔) **one** box.

 ☐

 ☐

 ☐

1.3 Complete the following **two** sentences by adding a number to each.

(2)

(a) In $\frac{9}{4}$ there are .... dotted-minim beats in a bar.

(b) A dotted-semiquaver is equal to .... demisemiquaver(s).

1.4 Tick (✔) **one** box to show which bar is grouped correctly.

(1)

☐

☐

☐

1.5 Tick (✔) **or** cross (✗) **each** box to show whether the rests are correct **or** incorrect.

(3)

☐   ☐   ☐

2.1 Tick (✔) **one** box to show the name of this note. (1)

 D ☐   C ☐   E ☐   A ☐

2.2 Tick (✔) **one** box to show the correct enharmonic equivalent of this note. (1)

    ☐    ☐    ☐

2.3 Here is a bar written for the horn in F. (5)

This bar has been transposed down a perfect 5th to be at sounding pitch. There are some mistakes. Put a tick (✔) **or** cross (✗) underneath the key signature and each note to show whether each is correct **or** incorrect.

☐   ☐   ☐ ☐ ☐

2.4 Compare bars **A**, **B** and **C**, then circle **TRUE** or **FALSE** for each of the **three** statements. (3)

A    B    C

(a) **A** and **C** are at the same pitch   **TRUE**   **FALSE**

(b) **A** is one octave higher than **B**   **TRUE**   **FALSE**

(c) **B** is one octave higher than **C**   **TRUE**   **FALSE**

3.1 Tick (✔) **one** box to show the correctly written key signature of G♯ minor.

(1)

3.2 Tick (✔) **one** box to show the correctly written key signature of D♭ major.

(1)

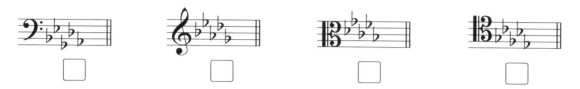

3.3 Circle the correct key of each of these **three** melodies.

(3)

(a) A major G♯ minor D major E major

(b) F major B♭ major G minor D minor

(c) C♯ minor G♯ minor D♯ minor F♯ minor

3.4 Tick (✔) **one box for X** and **one box for Y** to show which notes are needed
to complete the scale of **F♯ melodic minor**.

(2)

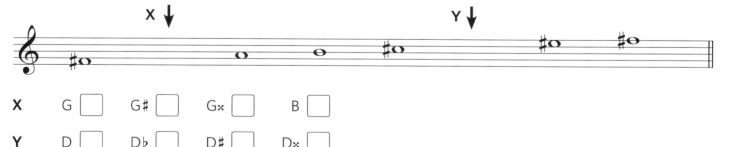

X   G ☐   G♯ ☐   G✕ ☐   B ☐

Y   D ☐   D♭ ☐   D♯ ☐   D✕ ☐

3.5 Circle **one** clef for each scale, to form **minor** scales.   (3)

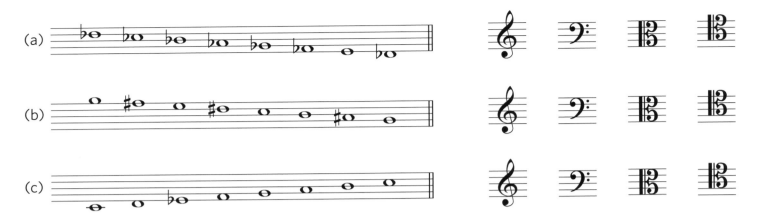

3.6 Circle **TRUE** or **FALSE** for each statement.   (2)

(a) This is the correctly written chromatic scale beginning on A♭   **TRUE**   **FALSE**

(b) This is the correctly written chromatic scale beginning on B   **TRUE**   **FALSE**

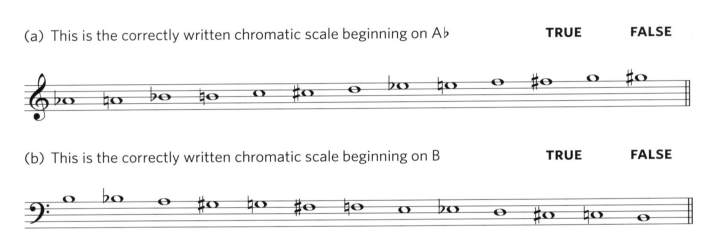

3.7 Circle **TRUE** or **FALSE** for each statement.   (3)

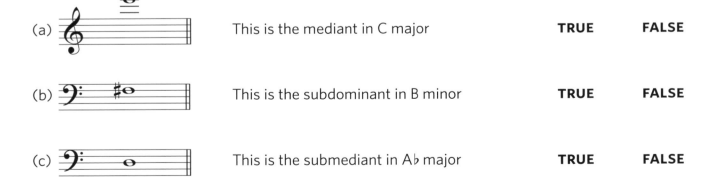

(a) This is the mediant in C major   **TRUE**   **FALSE**

(b) This is the subdominant in B minor   **TRUE**   **FALSE**

(c) This is the submediant in A♭ major   **TRUE**   **FALSE**

4.1 Tick (✔) **one** box to name each interval.

(3)

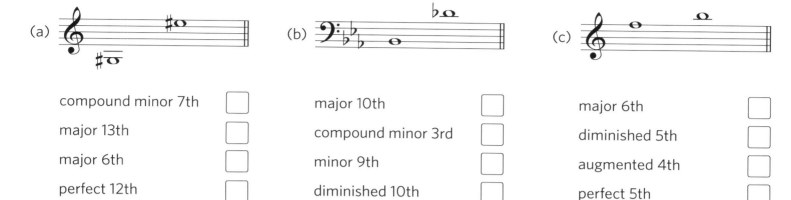

compound minor 7th ☐	major 10th ☐	major 6th ☐
major 13th ☐	compound minor 3rd ☐	diminished 5th ☐
major 6th ☐	minor 9th ☐	augmented 4th ☐
perfect 12th ☐	diminished 10th ☐	perfect 5th ☐

4.2 Circle the type of each interval.

(3)

(a) perfect   major   minor   diminished   augmented

(b) perfect   major   minor   diminished   augmented

(c) perfect   major   minor   diminished   augmented

4.3 Write notes to form the named intervals. Your note should be **higher** than the given note.

(4)

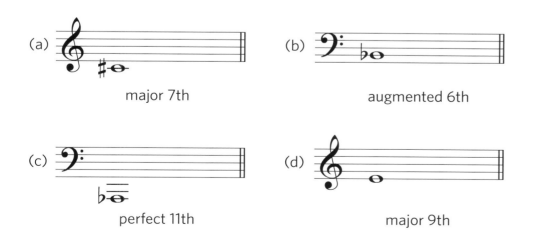

(a) major 7th

(b) augmented 6th

(c) perfect 11th

(d) major 9th

Turn the page

5 Chords

5.1 Indicate suitable chords for the two cadences in the following melody by writing either I, II, IV or V in each of the **five** boxes underneath the staves. (5)

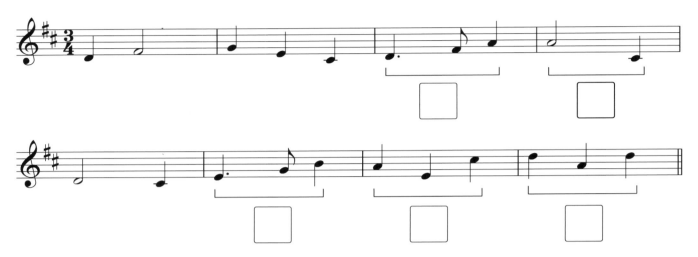

5.2 Tick (✔) **one** box to name each cadence. (2)

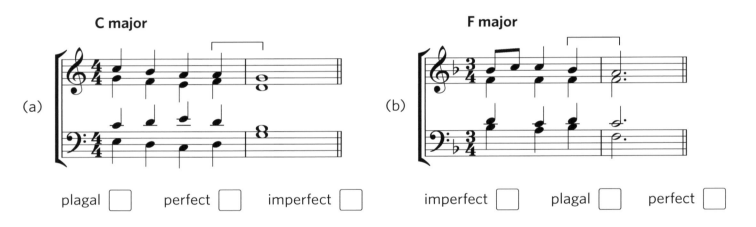

plagal ☐   perfect ☐   imperfect ☐   imperfect ☐   plagal ☐   perfect ☐

5.3 Tick (✔) one box to name each of the **three** marked chords. The key is G minor. (3)

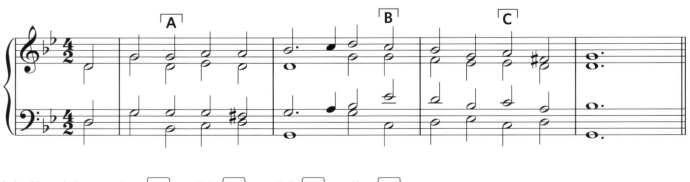

(a) Chord **A**   Ic ☐   IVa ☐   IVb ☐   Ib ☐

(b) Chord **B**   IVa ☐   IIb ☐   IIc ☐   IVc ☐

(c) Chord **C**   Ia ☐   IIb ☐   Va ☐   Vb ☐

6.1 Tick (✔) **one** box for each term/sign.

(3)

schnell means:

getting faster ☐

at a moderate speed ☐

slow ☐

fast ☐

attacca means:

at choice ☐

go straight on ☐

agitated ☐

broadly ☐

retenu means:

held back ☐

rather slow ☐

very slow ☐

pause on the note ☐

6.2 Tick (✔) one box to name each of the **two** written-out ornaments, which are marked with brackets.

(2)

(a)

turn ☐   trill ☐   upper mordent ☐   appoggiatura ☐

(b)

appoggiatura ☐   acciaccatura ☐   upper mordent ☐   turn ☐

6.3 Circle **TRUE** or **FALSE** for each of the following **five** statements.

(5)

(a) The triangle produces sounds of definite pitch   **TRUE**   **FALSE**

(b) The oboe is a transposing instrument   **TRUE**   **FALSE**

(c) The tuba is the lowest-sounding woodwind instrument   **TRUE**   **FALSE**

(d) The double bass might be played pizzicato   **TRUE**   **FALSE**

(e) The cor anglais is a double-reed instrument   **TRUE**   **FALSE**

Study this music for violin and piano and then answer the questions that follow.

7.1 Compare the following bars to bar 3 of the violin part, then tick (✔)
the **one** correct statement.

(1)

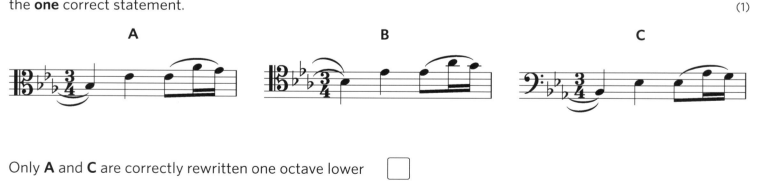

Only **A** and **C** are correctly rewritten one octave lower ☐

Only **C** is correctly rewritten one octave lower ☐

Only **B** and **C** are correctly rewritten one octave lower ☐

A, **B** and **C** are correctly rewritten one octave lower ☐

7.2 Circle **TRUE** or **FALSE** for each of the following **five** statements about the music. (5)

(a) The music should be played gracefully   **TRUE**   **FALSE**

(b) All of the notes in the violin part can be found in E♭ major   **TRUE**   **FALSE**

(c) The lowest note in the piano part is a G   **TRUE**   **FALSE**

(d) The smallest interval in the violin part of bars 1–4 is a major 2nd   **TRUE**   **FALSE**

(e) The ornament in the piano part of bar 7 is a turn   **TRUE**   **FALSE**

7.3 Which instrument is best suited to play the notes of the left-hand piano part in bars 1–4 so that they sound at the same pitch? Tick (✔) **one** box. (1)

oboe ☐   xylophone ☐   trumpet ☐   bassoon ☐

7.4 How many times does the **leading note** in the key of E♭ major appear in the left-hand part? Tick (✔) **one** box. (1)

2 ☐   3 ☐   4 ☐   5 ☐

7.5 Complete the following **two** sentences by adding a number to each. (2)

(a) There is an instruction to play a down-bow in bar ....

(b) The first note in the right-hand piano part of bar 4 is worth .... demisemiquavers.

Music Theory Sample Papers

ABRSM's official Music Theory Sample Papers are essential resources for candidates preparing for our Music Theory exams. They provide authentic practice material and are a reliable guide as to what to expect in the exam.

- Essential practice material for the new format ABRSM Grade 5 Theory exams
- Model answers also available

Support material for ABRSM Music Theory exams

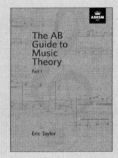

**Supporting the teaching and learning of music
in partnership with four Royal Schools of Music**

Royal Academy of Music | Royal College of Music
Royal Northern College of Music | Royal Conservatoire of Scotland

www.abrsm.org f facebook.com/abrsm
 @abrsm   ABRSM YouTube

ISBN 978-1-78601-359-0